# THE L·O·S·T
# ZOO

# THE L·O·S·T ZOO

## by · CHRISTOPHER · CAT
## and · COUNTEE · CULLEN

### illustrated by BRIAN PINKNEY

**Silver Burdett Press**
Englewood Cliffs
New Jersey

# DEDICATED

*(with Christopher's permission)*
*to the youngsters*
*one of us has taught*

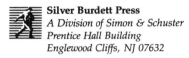

**Silver Burdett Press**
*A Division of Simon & Schuster*
*Prentice Hall Building*
*Englewood Cliffs, NJ 07632*

Copyright 1940 by Harper and Brothers,
Copyright © renewed 1968 by Ida M. Cullen,
copyright © 1990 by Amistad Inc. and administered by JHK/Cullen Associates.
This edition published in 1992 by Silver Burdett Press.

Manufactured in the United States of America.

Library of Congress Cataloging-in-Publication Data

Cullen, Countee.
    The lost zoo / Christopher Cat and Countee Cullen ; illustrated by
Brian Pinkney.
        p.    cm.
    Summary: Poems explain why one will not find such animals as the
Wakeupworld, the Squilililigee, the Sleepamitemore, and the Treasuretit in any
zoo we know.

    1. Animals, Mythical—Juvenile poetry.  2. Children's poetry, American.
[1. Animals, Mythical—Poetry.  2. Humorous poetry.  3. American poetry.]
I. Pinkney, J. Brian, ill.  II. Title. PS3505.U287L67  1991
811'. 52—dc20                                                       91-16532
                                                                         CIP
                                                                          AC

ISBN 0-382-24256-4 (hardcover)   ISBN 0-382-24255-6 (LSB)

123456789      969594939291
*Cover design by Antler & Baldwin, Inc.*

# C·O·N·T·E·N·T·S

# FOREWORD

The book you are holding is very special. It will make you laugh and it will make you wonder. It will spark your imagination as you create mind pictures of bees, fleas, snails, and other ordinary animals doing remarkable things. It will make you think twice the next time you see or read about some of the not-so-ordinary creatures such as lions, kangaroos, and dodo birds, that are included in this story. Most of all, it will teach you about some creatures that are so very extraordinary that you might never have heard about them at all were it not for this book.

THE LOST ZOO is a different version of the story of Noah's Ark. If you are familiar with the story you know that it was Noah's task to build an Ark, or boat, big enough to hold two each of all the animals in the land.

Imagine how big the Ark would have to be to hold all those animals, and how strong to protect the animals against forty days and nights of rain. This funny book is a retelling of how the animals came to be on that Ark—how the serious ones made it right on time, the lazy ones dillydallied until it was almost too late, and how some poor creatures never made it on board at all.

One of the many special things about this book is its authors. When you and I write stories, we generally write alone. Occasionally, when we share authorship with another writer, it is usually with a friend or someone else who is interested in the same topic or idea. Christopher Cat and Countee Cullen are indeed friends and they are interested in the same topics. Even so, most would say that this is an unusual writing partnership—cat and man. But if the collaboration works, and this one surely does, then that is all that counts.

Another special thing about this book is that it uses both regular story language, called prose, and poetry. The authors begin and end with prose. It is through prose that we get to know about their friendship. It is here that we are invited into the writing partnership, as we learn more about their warm and amusing relationship and how they work together. When the story of Noah's Ark begins, we shift from prose to poetry. Now, the language is so full of rhyme and rhythm that we almost want to sing it rather than say it.

Countee Cullen, the human half of this authorship team, wrote many poems and stories for children and adults. THE LOST ZOO was his first children's novel. He wanted to provide children with interesting books that would make them enjoy reading and want to read. As an

African-American youngster, Cullen spent much of his life in the Harlem section of New York City. As a young man, he studied both in the United States and in France, where he learned to speak and write French fluently. He taught English, French, and creative writing at Frederick Douglas Junior High School in New York City. Even as his fame grew as a writer, he continued to teach school, encouraging his students' writing talents and their love of literature. He loved the English language and took pride and pleasure in his ability to use it to bring joy and comfort to himself and others. The Countee Cullen Regional Library, a branch of the New York Public Library, was named in his honor.

This is a book that you will enjoy hearing read aloud. It is one that you will want to return to time and again to read by yourself or to share with a friend, taking turns reading to one another. Sometimes, you may simply want to choose certain parts to read aloud and talk about. Some of the more peculiar animals, those who did not make it on the Ark, may remind you of some people you know. You may want to create your own unusual animals and tell why they missed the Ark. You may even want to accept the challenge offered by Christopher Cat and Countee Cullen by creating your own version of what happened to certain animals in the story whose fate was left unclear. In order to do that, of course, you will first have to read on for yourself. So, read and enjoy.

Dorothy S. Strickland

# A WORD ABOUT CHRISTOPHER

**C**at is not only Christopher's last name, but Christopher *is* a cat, a real cat, colored white, and orangey. Christopher belongs to me, or maybe I belong to Christopher. That's what I often think sometimes, when I would like my easy chair to myself and have to share it with him. However, I don't think it matters now which of us belongs to the other. For I am sure that neither Christopher nor I would be very happy away from the other for a long time.

We have belonged to each other for a number of years, ever since Christopher was a kitten, and that wasn't yesterday. He is now a real honest-to-goodness sure-enough Cat, and you know how long it takes a kitten to become a Cat! I am only saying this to show how well Christopher and I know each other and how long we have been friends.

Now you, whoever you are, as you read what I am going to say about Christopher and me, will probably not want to believe what I am going to tell you. And there isn't any way in which I can make you believe me. I can only state the facts as they are, and hope that you *will* believe me. Well, here goes! Christopher and I understand one another. I don't mean that when I tell Christopher to get up and leave my easy chair to me that he will do so. I don't mean that when I ask him, nicely and politely, to show off in front of company by washing behind his ears for me, or by nipping me gently on the elbow or on the kneecap (as he often does when we are alone), that he will do it. Oh, no, not Christopher! The

very time I want him to do something clever, that's the very time he pretends to be the most unintelligent cat on earth. When I say that Christopher and I understand each other, I mean that we have known one another so long that each of us truly knows what the other is talking about. We have invented a kind of man-cat language that each of us knows, and we're pretty proud of it. Not everybody who has a cat can do that, neither can every cat who has a master.

It shouldn't be too surprising though, that Christopher and I can talk to one another. For after you have lived in the same house with a person, or animal, it doesn't matter which, for almost ten years, and after you've both met every morning for breakfast, and every evening for dinner, and every night you've both climbed into the same easy chair, and fallen asleep together right after dinner, it shouldn't be surprising that you two finally ended up talking to one another. Well, that's how it is with Christopher and me.

Up to a short time ago Christopher and I had never really had much serious conversation. It had usually been no more than "Good morning" in the morning, or "Hello, you back?" at night. Sometimes Christopher might ask, "How was work today? Did you have a nice day?" But as he seldom waited for an answer, I suppose those questions were just for the sake of politeness, and that he really didn't care how my day had been. Usually after supper we were both too sleepy and too well-filled to think of carrying on any kind of exciting talk, although we might quarrel a little about the easy chair. I might say, "Christopher, there are at least four other chairs in this room. This chair is mine, and I don't see why you don't choose another one." And Christopher might answer, and he might not, all depending on how he was feeling at the time. If he did answer, it would only be to deny my right to my own chair. So I have finally become accustomed to sharing my slumber seat with Christopher, as he slyly works himself through the sides of the chair, little by little shoves me over to one side, and eases himself into a position of comfort. I think I should miss him if he weren't there beside me softly purring every night.

But although we didn't talk much, we knew that we *could* talk to one another, and that was a great deal of comfort. We could begin anytime we wanted to. And the chance for a real heart-to-heart or cat-to-man talk came not so long ago.

Christopher isn't the only animal I like, although I probably like him more than any other animal I'm acquainted with at the present time. The fact is that I like animals in general. I like to look at them. They always astonish me. I am never sure of what they are going to do, and I am constantly being surprised. Now if you're that kind of person (as I am), a good place to go (as often as you like), is the Zoo. And that's where I go any number of times.

For a long while I didn't let on to Christopher about these visits, because I thought he might begin to worry me about taking *him*, and I didn't see how I could do that. It would have been all right if he had been a dog, for then I could have put a strap on him and kept him in hand. But cats are different. They are very independent, and you never know what they are going to do. To be sure, once in France I did see a cat walking at his master's side in a very intelligent manner, out for an airing, just as you or I, or anyone else, might go out for one; but that was a French cat, and it may be that French cats are a little easier to handle than American cats. (I must ask Christopher what he thinks about that sometime.)

As I said before, for a long time I didn't tell Christopher about my trips to the Zoo, but one day I had had just too fine a time to keep it all to myself. The monkeys had never been funnier; the lions had roared like mad; in the bird house there was such singing as I had never heard before. In fact, all the animals at whose cages I had stopped had behaved just as if they were doing a circus act for me alone. I had to tell someone. And I decided to tell Christopher.

So right after dinner I began. "Christopher," I said, very softly. We were both in the same chair, so I didn't see any reason to speak in a loud tone of voice. I'm sure he heard me the first time, but he didn't answer, just kept his eyes shut, and went on purring softly to himself. It was quite plain that he wasn't in the mood for after-dinner chatter. But I was bubbling over, and I wanted to talk.

I bent down and spoke right into his ear. "Christopher," I said, as distinctly as I could, "wake up; I want to talk to you."

He flicked his ears at me, parted his lips and yawned at me, pointing a very tiny pink tongue at me, and then he opened one very yellow and sleepy eye. "Must you?" he said.

"Must I what, Christopher?" I asked, not understanding his reply.

"Must you talk?" he replied. "I really don't care to; I'd much rather sleep. I have a feeling in my bones that the day after tomorrow is going to be a rainy day. That means that tomorrow I'll have to be jumping and running like a demon to indicate that there will be rain the day after tomorrow. I'd really like to sleep, so I'll be in good shape."

"I don't care, Christopher," I exclaimed, for I was just a little bit annoyed. "It isn't often that I ask you to talk to me, and I think you might do it pleasantly and without any fuss, if for no other reason than the fact that you're sitting in my chair."

"Well," said Christopher rising and arching his back, "if that's the way you feel about it, I suppose there is nothing for me to do but talk to you. Did you enjoy your dinner tonight? To be quite frank with you, I thought my liver was a little tough."

"I don't want to talk about dinner, Christopher. I have something really exciting to talk about. This afternoon, where do you think I went?"

"Oh," said Christopher, his yellow eyes widening in astonishment, "didn't you go to work?"

"Yes, yes, of course I did, but I mean later. I went somewhere else. Where do you think? Come on, guess!"

"I give up," purred Christopher contentedly, without making even the slightest attempt to guess. "Tell me. Where *did* you go?"

"To the Zoo!" I answered very importantly, looking him straight in the eye to see how he would take it, for I was sure he would be beside himself with excitement!

You can imagine my disappointment when all he said was, "Oh, *that* place!"

"Is that all you have to say, Christopher?"

"No," he answered, gazing at me sadly. "How I pity all those poor animals."

"Now, Christopher," I tried to explain to him, "we couldn't very well have them walking up and down the

14

street rubbing elbows with people, could we?"

"I don't see why not," he argued stubbornly. "If people didn't annoy *them*, I am sure *they* would be very polite, and that all of them would mind their own affairs, and the world would be much more interesting than it is now. And don't tell me that they would bite people and scratch them. I am sure they would do nothing of the sort, if they were let alone. Anything will bite and scratch if you annoy it. You know I can scratch, myself, don't you?" And here he put forth his claws which certainly did look very, very sharp. "And I can bite, too," he went on. And here he opened his mouth as wide as he could.

I really wanted to laugh at him then, for most of his teeth are so tiny that they look quite harmless, although he does have some long side teeth which appear a bit more frightening than the others. He waved his little pink tongue at me in a very dangerous manner.

"Would you really bite me, Christopher?" I asked, pretending an anxiety which I am sure he was able to see through.

Christopher's face broke into the loveliest smile as he rubbed his head against the back of my hand. "You goose," he laughed, "you know I wouldn't. We never bite people we like."

"Why, Christopher!" I exclaimed. "That's the first time you've ever told me you liked me!"

"Oh, no, it isn't," he shook his head. "I've told you many, many times, only you haven't known it, just because I didn't come right out and say so. Every time I rub up against your trousers (sometimes even rubbing so hard that my fur comes off on your trousers leg), every time I jump up in the chair beside you, every time I lie still and permit you to rub my head, I'm telling you that I like you. You must have noticed that I don't treat everyone that way."

"Well, yes," I had to admit, "I have noticed that."

"Then that proves that I like you," said Christopher. "But about your trip to the Zoo this afternoon. What did you do there and what did you see?"

"Aha, I thought you'd be interested," I teased him. "Well, first I went to the monkey house, and what antics they put on for me! I don't know when I have laughed so much. Then I wandered over to the lions' house and watched those majestic animals. There was one in particular, Christopher, who reminded me very much of you, except that he was so much bigger."

"Probably a cousin of mine," Christopher replied lightly. "You know we Cats and Lions are distantly related. But it seems to me that you didn't see anything or anyone very exciting. Wasn't there anything new?"

"Such as what, Christopher?"

He had been lying on his back all this time, gently nibbling at one of my fingers while talking. Now he gave my finger a final lick with his rough little tongue, and then he sat up, quite erect and faced me. His eyes had a sly, laughing look in them, as if he were enjoying a huge joke, and something made me feel that I was that joke.

"Did you, by any chance," he asked, "see a Squilililigee?"

"Did I see a Squilly What?" I sputtered.

Christopher placed his head between his two front paws and shook with merriment. "Oh, I knew you wouldn't be able to say it," he laughed. "But did you see a Squilililigee?"

"No, Christopher," I replied, as calmly as I could. "No, I didn't see a Squilililigee."

"You bet you didn't, and you bet you never will," said Christopher, and he began to laugh again, so heartily that he almost rolled from our chair.

After he had caught his breath again, he wanted to know: "Did you see a twelve-eyed Wakeupworld?"

"No, Christopher," I replied. "I didn't see a twelve-eyed Wakeupworld."

"You bet you didn't, and you bet you never will," he went on, just as before. "How about a Treasuretit? Did you see one of those?"

"No, Christopher," I said, "I didn't see a Treasuretit."

"You bet you didn't see one," he echoed. "Now how about a Lapalake? Did you see one of those?"

"No, Christopher," I said quietly, "I not only didn't see a Lapalake, but I never in all my life heard of one before."

"You bet you didn't," he continued teasing me. "And I bet you didn't see a One-sided Lopsided Lizard, or a Snake-That-Walked-Upon-His-Tail, or a Sleepamitemore, or a Double-Headed Hoodinkus, or a Ha-Ha-Ha!"

"Oh," I interrupted, certain that I was going to get the better of him at last, "if you mean a laughing Hyena, then you are wrong, for I did see one of those."

"But I don't mean a laughing Hyena," said Christopher slowly and evenly, as if talking to a very stupid person. "A Hyena is one thing and a Ha-Ha-Ha is another thing, and I meant a Ha-Ha-Ha. When I say a Ha-Ha-Ha, I don't mean a Hyena, and when I say a Hyena, I don't mean a Ha-Ha-Ha, or vice versa. Now, did you see a Ha-Ha-Ha?"

I answered weakly, "No, Christopher, I did not see a Ha-Ha-Ha."

"You bet you didn't, and you bet you never will," he said with an air of closing the subject, "because there aren't any more; no more merry Ha-Ha-Has, no more contrary Double-Headed Hoodinkuses, no more lazy Sleepamitemores, and no more proud Snake-That-Walked-Upon-His-Tail, no more One-sided Lopsided Lizards, no more thirsty Lapalakes, no more beautiful Wakeupworlds with eyes like rainbows, and no more sad little Squilililigees!" Here Christopher sighed deeply and curled himself up into a ball as if to sleep.

Now, if he thought that I was going to permit him to fall asleep after he had made me as curious as I now was, he was greatly mistaken. I shook him wide awake at once.

"Oh, no, you don't," I exclaimed. "You can't go to

18

sleep now. You've got to explain all these funny animals you've been asking me about. What are they? And why won't I ever have a chance to see them? And why won't there ever be any more of them? I'm still young, and the world is full of Zoos, and I can go from Zoo to Zoo until I find all these animals, or, if I am obliged to do so, I can even go into the jungles and look for them." (I don't believe I really meant that last statement, for I don't believe I would like going into the jungles to hunt for anything, let alone a lot of animals I'd never heard of; I don't think I'd like that at all, but since I had said it, I couldn't take it back, so I just put on my bravest look.)

"You poor, poor fellow," said Christopher sadly. "Neither money nor courage, nor anything men possess, can get you a look at those animals. They all died thousands of years ago; there have never been any more; and there never will be. They were all drowned."

"But how, Christopher, *how*, please tell me HOW?

Christopher reached over and patted me with a little paw so soft you couldn't guess that sharp claws were hidden beneath. "Now, now, now," he said, "don't excite yourself. I'll tell you all about it."

And then every night, for many, many nights Christopher told me of those animals we shall never see again, the animals of THE LOST ZOO, who didn't get into Noah's Ark, even though he sent them all invitations. The story came to Christopher from his father, who had it from his father, who had it from his father, and on and on back to the very first of all the Christopher Cats, the one who was in Noah's Ark. When I had heard the whole story, I told Christopher that I thought the boys and girls of the world ought to know about it; and he agreed with me, and gave me his permission to write the story in my

*19*

own way. That's what he said, that I could write it in my own way, but I suppose he seldom means what he says, for all the time I was writing, he was forever bringing me ideas of his own which he said ought to go in. Sometimes I thought they were good, but most of the time I didn't think they had quite enough to do with what I was writing. However, as I felt that I owed Christopher something for telling me the story, I suggested that what he had to say go at the bottom of the page as footnotes. This suggestion pleased him mightily because it made him look like a scholar. That's why all the footnotes in this book have Christopher's name in front of them. I don't claim any credit for them; good or bad those little verses all belong to Christopher.

What happened later only goes to show that no matter how close you are to a cat, you can never read all a cat's thoughts. When the book was finally completed I showed it to Christopher.

"There, Christopher," I said, happily, "there we are, all finished, and you don't know how much I appreciate your part in this book. You shall have an extra supply of catnip, milk, and liver from now on."

"That's all very well," replied Christopher in an icy tone which utterly surprised me, "but I am not interested in catnip, milk, and liver just now. I want to be an author. I deserve to be an author—at least half an author; for you would never have written this book if I hadn't told you the story, and I think the least you can do is to let the whole world know it by giving me half the credit. They could make the print a little smaller and put both our names on the same page.

I must confess that I was astonished. Such a thing had never entered my head. A cat, as part author of a book? Whoever in the world had heard of such a thing?

Christopher must have read my mind. "Now don't go telling me that you never heard of such a thing," he said, shaking a paw at me. "That's what you people always say when you don't want to do the fair thing by us animals. *You never heard of such a thing!* You never heard of those lost animals either until I told you of them; but that didn't keep you from writing about them. And although it may surprise people at first to see my name on a book, they'll gradually get used to it."

There wasn't anything I could say to such a straightforward argument. I gave in as gracefully as I could, and so Christopher's name appears (as it should!) along with mine as half-author of this book.

You've heard, no doubt, of the Dinosaur,
The Dodo bird, and the African Roc;
But the Wakeupworld, shaped like a clock,
And the lazy Sleepamitemore,
The Pussybow that could mew and bark,
The lonely Squililligee,
The Treasuretit that loved the dark,
Nobody's heard of these but me![1]
The-Snake-That-Walked-Upon-His-Tail,
(The female couldn't, just the male.)
The Ha-Ha-Ha with constant grin,
Hoodinkus, single yet a twin,
These are a few (and only a few)
Of the left-out ones who missed the Ark
Tall as a mountain and broad as a park
To which all had been invited (to).[2]

When Noah was bidden, "Build an Ark
Tall as a mountain and broad as a park,
Against the time the rains descend
For forty days without an end,
And summon the animals two by two
Of every size and shape and hue!"
He wondered mightily what to do.
How should he ever get them word,
How tell each fish, each beast, each bird,
A message send to hive and den,
To every animal living then?

[1] CHRISTOPHER: And me!

[2] CHRISTOPHER: I raise not one minutest mew
Of praise for such a line, nor clamor
For kinship with an author who
Makes use of such unlawful grammar.

How should he ever get them in,
Each hoof and wing, each claw and fin?

Though he was known as a nimble wit,
This was a task, you will admit,
Demanding thought of great degree.
Though you who read may be quite clever,
I have grave doubts if ever, ever,
You could have done as well as he!

Unhappy Noah, with mind askew,
He scratched his head as thinkers do,
When, quick as a thought, fast as a wish,
Came this advice: "Don't ask the *fish!*
Leave it to them to sink or swim!"
Which was, I think, most clever of him.

O happy Noah, happy, happy he!
Despite his asthma and his age,
For such a venerable sage
He capered most amazingly!
Since not a fish he need invite, he
Need not pack the rest so tightly
Into his wonderful, marvelous bark
Tall as a mountain and broad as a park!

"I'm good at making things," quoth he,
"So the Ark is a matter of one, two, three."
"But never," he groaned, his fingers biting,
"Have I been much at letter writing.
Yet I was never one to shirk
A necessary bit of work!"

And so with a pint or two of ink,
With paper by the quire and ream,
He soberly sat down to think,
To bite his pen, and dream and dream.

In later years he often said,
Shaking a gray and thoughtful head,
"The more I thought, the farther flew
The thoughts I'd set my thinking to,
Till just as I'd decided I'd
Find someone who for love or pelf,
Would ride this horse I couldn't ride,
That letter up and wrote itself:

25

"To each dear beast,
Largest and least,
Beasts of the forest,
Beasts of the fen,
Beasts of the marshes,
Of wood, and of glen,
Animals small,
Animals tall,
Animals webbed and furry;
Hear ye!
Appear ye!
Hurry!
Scurry!
By that decision
That fits your tribe,
With thought and with vision,
By election,
Selection,
By trial and error,
By gift or by bribe,
In some sort of way,
Choose for the day
That draws nearer and nearer,
Two of your troop
To ride on the sloop
I'm building to save
A few of you from a watery grave!
For a month from today,
And not a day more,
The skies will give way,
And how it will pour!

Oh, not the small shower
That lasts for an hour,
Nor the heavier fall
That comes with a squall,
And is suddenly over!

To weather a week of
Rain's nothing to speak of;
But rain that will cover
A forty day span,
Why who can recall
A like waterfall
In the memory of man?
Prepare for this wetting
The world will be getting,
And let us save those that we can!

The trip will not bore you
Of that I assure you;
Every measure
To heighten your pleasure
Will surely be tried.
Our decks are capacious,
And certainly spacious
Enough for an L. E. Phant's stride.
We'll breakfast at seven,
With broth at eleven,
Drink tea at a quarter past four;
At eight such a dinner!
We'll wish we were thinner,
For then we might all ask for more!

And all sorts of things
To make it the pleasantest cruise.
And (you'll never guess!)
I've even a press
Each day to supply us with news!

So please don't be losing
A moment in choosing
Your delegates two.
Their cards of admission
I herewith enclose;
Unless they have those,
No other condition
Will usher them through.

So anxiously waiting,
And anticipating
A capital trip
On my capital ship,
On my beautiful, bonny, brave bark,

Yours: Noah, who just built the Ark."

Then, what a hustling
There was! What a bustling
And getting together!
Such a chit-chatter
Over the matter;
Every beast talked of the weather![1]

[1] CHRISTOPHER: Which really was silly;
For what was there to gain,
Since, willy-nilly,
It was bound to rain?

In council and meeting,
Assembly and forum,
They were busy completing
A requisite quorum.

And, little time losing,
They set about choosing
(All by majority vote)
Two of each kind,
The best they could find,
For passage on Noah's big boat.

But no beast had a chance to live
Who was not quite superlative.

They chose the *largest* L. E. Phants;
They chose the *most industrious* Ants;
With dispositions mild and sunny,
Those Bees that made the *purest* honey;
The Lions with the *loudest* roar;
Those Eagles which could *highest* soar;
The Fleas that could the *farthest* jump;
The Camels with the *biggest* hump;
The Tigers with the *strongest* teeth,
And *sharpest* claws, soft pads beneath;
The two Giraffes with *longest* strides;
Rhinoceri with *toughest* hides;
The Donkeys which were *balkiest;*
The Parrots which were *talkiest;*
The Monkeys with the *curliest* tails;
The *sweetest-singing* Nightingales;
The *slyest* Foxes; *slowest* Snails;
The *fleetest* Deer with *saddest* eyes;
Of every clan they chose the prize.

Of Cats they chose the Christophers
Because these had the *sleekest* furs,
The *finest* whiskers, *trimmest* claws,
The *proudest* tails, the *prettiest* paws,
And eyes far brighter in the dark
Than any Jack o'Lantern spark.
Each tribe, each group, North, South,
    East, West,
Was subject to the *strictest* test,
And none was chosen but the *best*.

Next morning, early, oh, so early,
While still the grass was wet and pearly,
The Kangaroo and Pelican
(One from his pouch, one from his bill)
More answers than might swell a van
Threw in at Noah's windowsill.

"Now here," said Noah, as he scanned
The many missives in his hand,
"Now here's complaining
By tens and scores;
It isn't raining,
And yet it pours!"
(He looked around
As he uttered that,
But his Mrs. frowned,
And his joke fell flat.)[1]

[1] CHRISTOPHER: As jokes of husbands often do
When wives are those they tell them to.

31

# FIRST CAME L.E. PHANT'S LETTER

DEAR NOAH: Please save me a spot
Exposed to the sun, where the Mice are *not*;
But if I *must* share my chamber, the Ant
Is the one I should welcome. Yours: L. E. Phant.[1]

[1] CHRISTOPHER: It's a notion quite compelling
       That he wasn't good at *spelling!*

# THEN CAME ATOM'S ANSWER

DEAR NOAH: To lend a flavor
Of fun to the trip,
As a special favor
Arrange to slip
Me in the L. E. Phant's cage.
My, won't he rage!
He'll prance and he'll leap,
And shake your big house,
When he finds he's to sleep
Near Atom, the Mouse.

# AND THIS FROM BRUIN BEAR

As I must have honey
If I am to thrive,
Please see that you lodge me
Close to a hive.
I'll be ever so careful,
And try not to ruin
The tiniest Bee.
Yours faithfully: Bruin.

# NEXT, FROM THE BEES

Dear Noah: A rumor
Says we are to share
Our hive (and our honey!)
With Bruin the Bear!
We here go on record,
(We'd go on our knees
If Bees *had* knees)
As being opposed
To plans such as these.
Busily yours: the Bees.

# AND LEO LION'S LINES

Please bear in mind my royal descent;
As King of them all, I believe I was meant
To have private quarters completely my own,
Attendants a few, a crown, and a throne.
*Noblesse oblige*, which means I rely on
You to oblige me: Leo the Lion.

# AND . . .

Last of the lot, though far from least,
And signed by many a thoughtless beast,
Bulky and broad with discontent
Like a legal draft or document,
At the bottom lay, on harmless mission,
This sinister and base petition:

> *Dear* Noah: (It began)
> Dear *Noah:* (So it ran)
> *Dear Noah:* We've heard
> From reliable source,
> (It sounds quite absurd
> To us, but of course
> There's never no telling[1]
> What people will do
> With only *their* comfort
> And quiet in view)
> That our shipmate-to-be,
> On your marvelous junk,
> Is none other than Sammie,
> Yes, Sammie, the Skunk!
> We all think it best
> Emphatically
> At once to protest,
> Vociferously,
> Against such company!
> Herewith attested,

[1] CHRISTOPHER: There's never *any* telling
Is more correct to say,
But grammar and spelling
Were young in Noah's day.

Duly protested,
And signed:
Hazel Hind,
Atom Ant,
L. E. Phant,
Michael Monkey,
Donald Donkey,
Billie Goat,
Stephen Shoat,
Cora Cow,
Sally Sow,
Alfred Auk,
Herbert Hawk,
Mamie Mouse,
Lucy Louse,
Gertie Grouse,
Benjamin Bull,
Gracie Gull,
Ronald Ram,
Leonard Lamb,
Freddie Frog,
Harry Hog,
Dannie Dog,
Bobbie Bat,
Christopher Cat,[1]
Rufus Rat,
Gnewton Gnat,
Fannie Flea,
Beulah Bee,

[1] CHRISTOPHER: That Christopher was first of my line;
They'd never have made the present one sign;
For apart from being a mighty fine cat,
I am absolutely a democrat!

*38*

Oscar Ox,
Francis Fox,
Mabel Moose,
George G. Goose,
Eunice Ewe,
Gnora Gnu,
Henry Hare,
Bruin Bear,
Ernest Elk,
Gussie Gazelk,[1]
Quincy Quail,
Sarah Snail,
Eddie Eagle,
Bessie Beagle,
Buster Baboon,
Richard Raccoon,
Douglas Duck,
Willie Woodchuck,
Adolphus Armadillo,
Gregory Gorilla,
Karl Kangaroo,
Ken Karibou,
Robert Rhinoceros,
Harold Hippotomus,[2]

And many others, oh shame of shames,
Who never learned to write their names!
(Of course there were some whose dignity

[1] CHRISTOPHER: Gussie just *would* spell it like that!

[2] CHRISTOPHER: That's how he spelled it then,
As all good scholars know;
He was much stouter when
He added the extra *po.*

Would never permit their names to be
Part of a petition
Under *any* condition!)

But straight behind this letter came
Another bearing Sammie's name:

DEAR NOAH: The slander
And rank propaganda[1]
Going the rounds about me,
Have enlargened my dander
To an appalling degree!
Though some I've detested,
Their customs protested,
I have never molested
One animal wantonly.
I'm perfectly able
To sit down at table
With elegant company;
I've a joke and a fable,
And tell them most cleverly;
My patience is a virtue,
And I'd never hurt you
Or any one willfully,
Of my equipment defensive,
Be not apprehensive!
As long as no harm's done to me,
May my sorrows be doubled,
And my tribe all be sunk,
If you're worried or troubled
By: Sammie the Skunk.

[1] CHRISTOPHER: From Sammie's rhyming 'tis easily seen
How English his accent must have bean!

40

P.S.
That here's a chance, I hope you'll see,
Forevermore for you to be
The Father of Democracy.
Come, show the world that you've got spunk,
By being just to: Sammie Skunk!

Old Noah smiled as he paced his decks,
Old Noah smiled as he wiped his specs.

"A right nice letter that," said Noah;
"The hand's as round and full as a dollar;
Its tone and composition show a
Spirit fine, and the mind of a scholar.
What if your fellows shrink from you,
O wise and witty Sammie Skunk?
Be fellowship between us two;
Come on, and share your Captain's bunk!"

How brightly luminuous
The fatal day arose!
No darkly ominous
Cloud the clear sky shows;
But blue, blue, blue, so blue,
The fields of Heaven lay,
Almost the eye looked through
At angels gay at play;
Almost the flowers there
You saw, and Heaven's trees,
Heard music, Heaven's air,
Drift through the gentle breeze.
On such a day, so rich with hope,

Without a hint of pain,
How could the smiling Heavens open
On forty days of rain?

But, nothing daunted, Noah strode
The decks of his mighty Ark;
Clear for all his signal showed:
"Embark you! All, embark!"

Then down they sped to the water's edge,
Through tree and grass, over hill and hedge;
Of every kind came two.
And up they went, up, up the plank,
Beast after beast; rank after rank
Went up, and on, and through,
Without punching or slapping,
Without pinching or scrapping,
(No snatching of banners)[1]
Without shoving or pushing,
Without jostling or rushing,
(Each minding his manners)[1]
Without hissing or snarling,
Without fighting or quarreling,
(No breaking the line!)
Without any endeavor
To be rude or to be clever,
The delegates all were fine![1]

Some wept to leave their mothers,
Their fathers, sisters, brothers,
Their joyous, lively friends;
(But eyes grow weary weeping,

[1] CHRISTOPHER: I do hope some one mentions
This to certain Conventions!

And find release in sleeping,
Till even weeping ends.)

The banks on either side were lined
With millions doomed to stay behind,
And find a billowy grave;
But each beast standing straight and strong
To speed the chosen ones along,
Tried hard to show him brave.

One minor incident there was
Which caused the delegates to buzz
With righteous indignation:
(For beasts, like men, can always show
A few who ever fall below
In any situation.)

The Kangaroos were gently wending
Their way along, the plank ascending,
When, seeing how they lurched,
When, grown suspicious of a gait
Not quite in keeping with their weight,
The Skipper had them searched!

He had their pouches opened wide,
And what so tightly packed inside
Did such a search reveal,
But six small cousins whom the chosen,
Now standing dumbly shamed and frozen,
Had wanted to conceal!

"Shame! Shame!" cried all the others,
"For we have kinsmen too;

We've fathers and mothers,
And sisters and brothers,
And cousins,
By dozens,
But such a *bad* thing,
But such a *mad* thing,
We *never* would do!"

The little Kangaroos were yanked
Forthwith from those pouches,
And, having been quite roundly spanked,
Dismissed with "oh's" and "ouches."
Their cousins twain, with shame to fleck
Their faces, hopped below;
Nor were they seen on the upper deck
For nearly a week or so!

Now, though a line from here to yonder
May stretch, until at length we wonder
If ever it will end,
We *know* that it will end.

So if the early bird was fast,
And first of all to sail,
You may be sure the very last
Were Mr. and Mrs. Snail!
But in they were, with Noah to thank,
Free from the coming tide.
Now up, high up, up with the plank,
And off for a forty day ride,
With animals twain from every clan
Known to the nimble mind of man,
All safe and sound inside!

# EXCEPT THESE VERY UNFORTUNATE
# FEW WE NEVER SHALL SEE IN ANY ZOO

# THE WAKEUPWORLD

This was the song of the Wakeupworld,
The beautiful beast with long tail curled:

*'Wake up, O World; O World, awake!*
*The light is bright on hill and lake;*
*O World, awake; wake up, O World!*
*The flags of the wind are all unfurled;*
*Wake up, O World; O World, awake!*
*Of earth's delightfulness partake.*

*Wake up, O World, whatever hour;*
*Sweet are the fields, sweet is the flower!*
*Wake up, O World; O World, awake;*
*Perhaps to see the daylight break,*
*Perhaps to see the sun descend,*
*The night begin, the daylight end.*

47

*But something surely to behold,*
*Not bought with silver or with gold,*
*Not shown in any land of dreams.*
*For open eyes the whole world teems*
*With lovely things to do or make,*
*Wake up, O World; O World, awake!"*

Such was the song of the Wakeupworld,
The beautiful beast with long tail curled,
The Wakeupworld so swift and fleet,
With twelve bright eyes and six strong feet.
Such was the song he sang all day,
Lest man or beast should sleep away
The gift of Time, and never know
The beauties of this life below.
Twelve were his eyes, as I have said,
Placed clockwise in his massive head.
Never in any time or weather
Were all those eyes shut tight together,
But daily, at its certain hour,
Each eye became possessed of power.

At one, an eye all pale and white
Flew open for the day's first sight,
And looked alone, until at two
There woke his wondering eye of blue.
His eye of green at stroke of three
Blazed like a jewel brilliantly;
At four he opened up the red,
And all around its luster spread.
Shyly then, as if all sleepy yet,
At five peeped forth the violet.
An eye of silver, chill and cold,

The hour of six would then unfold.
At seven with a sudden wink,
He would let loose his eye of pink.
At eight an eye so mild and mellow
Would gaze about; this one was yellow.
Prompt at the stroke of nine they say
Would twinkle forth his eye of gray.
At ten, as merry as a clown,
You could behold the laughing brown.
Eleven strikes! And open flies
An eye as black as midnight skies.
And when the hour of twelve was tolled,
And Time was one more half day old,
He opened full his eye of gold.
His twelve bright eyes he flashed around
Till rainbows flecked the trees and ground!
Oh, loveliest beast in song or story,
The Wakeupworld in all his glory!

He could not sleep as others could;
But for a moment in the wood
Might stand and rest himself a mite,
Then quickly would be off in flight,
Crossing mountain, field, and lake,
Bidding the drowsy world awake.
Every hour some sleepyhead
Would hear his song and leap from bed[1]
To open his eyes on some delight
Of lovely day or beauteous night.

---

[1] CHRISTOPHER: That is, all would, except that bore,
That lazy one, that Sleepamitemore,
Who still would sleep and snore and snore!

What would *you* give to see alive
A Wakeupworld at half past five?
Could anything excite you more
Than seeing him at exactly four,
His eyes of white, blue, green, and red,
Leaping like car lights from his head?
Or watch each eye from hour to hour,
Beginning at exactly one,
Unfold its beauty like a flower,
Till all those eyes were on the sun?
'Twould take you half a day at least
To get the most of such a feast![1]
But never shall his like appear
Again, and we shall never hear
His song in lovely measures hurled
At sleepyheads throughout the world.

Excitement robbed him of his breath,
Excitement led him to his death.
Flood morning when he could have been
(Being awake) the first one in,
Excitement made him play the dunce
And open all his eyes at once!
He rushed right on through dawn and dark
Pointing late comers to the Ark.
Too great the strain was for his heart;
Slowly he sank; his great knees shook,
While those his song had helped to start
Passed on without a backward look.

[1] CHRISTOPHER: He'd be the prize of any Zoo,
                 If he were here, I think, don't you?

50

The waters fell upon him there,
His twelve bright eyes shining like one;
They covered him, and none knew where
To find him when the storm was done.

# THE SQUILILILIGEE

He was the gentlest creature made;
Alone he lived, and alone he played,
    Ever so quietly.
He would have made the nicest pet,
But now there's no place one may get
    A Squilililigee.

Never an animal half so shy,
With such a sad and lonesome eye,
    The world will ever see;
With spotted fur all brown and yellow,
He was a most attractive fellow,
    The Squilililigee.

He would have eaten from your hand,
Fetched sticks and stones at your command,
    Quite agreeably;
He would have run close by your side,
Happy at heart, though lonesome-eyed,
    The Squilililigee.

He had a little tufted tail,
And held it high just like a sail
    When things went merrily,
Waved it in such a gladsome manner
It seemed a brown and yellow banner—
    Did Squilililigee.

But if perchance his pride were hurt,
That merry flag drooped in the dirt
    Quite distressfully,
And tears as large and wet as those
*You* ever shed rolled down the nose
    Of Squilililigee!

If only when the moment came
For naming him, some other name
    His had been, happily
He never would have missed the Ark,

And we might have in every park
    A Squilililigee!

But he was fated from the start
To have a most unhappy heart,
    Broken easily;
He never had an answer pert
For others when his pride was hurt—
    Shy Squilililigee.

And all his saddest moments came
Because he had so strange a name;
    For what could better be
For any tongue or mouth to say
In tones ridiculous and gay
    Than: SQUILILILIGEE!

Now just suppose that you, or you,
Instead of the name you answer to
    So importantly,
Shuddered to hear your name at all,
Because it boomed like a waterfall,
    Like: SQUILILILIGEE!

Now, Tiger is a pleasant name,
And Bear, and L. E. Phant the same;
    On that we all agree;
Armadillo, likewise Giraffe;
But everyone of us must laugh
    At SQUILILILIGEE!

And thus his name became a joke
Whenever it was heard or spoke

In any company,
Till he grew shyer by the hour,
His nature just a trifle sour,
    Poor Squilililigee!

Whenever mischief had been done
Under the moon or under the sun,
    The forest instantly
(Because they loved to say his name)
Would shout in laughing tones: Oh, shame
    On Squilililigee!

Was something missing? Where did it go?
Who was the thief? Did anyone know?
    How gleefully
Came answer from a thousand throats
In gurgles, chuckles, and merry notes:
"'Twas SQUILILILIGEE!"

Not that they thought he did such things,
But just for the pleasure teasing brings;
    (No, not spitefully,)
But just to see him blush with shame
They thundered forth that funny name:
    SQUILILILIGEE!

Such was the state of keen distress
In which he lived in loneliness
    A little bitterly,
When into his possession came
A letter signed with Noah's name;
    To: SQUILILILIGEE!

He gazed at Noah's invitation;
"Relief," said he, "from my sad station
    In this note I see;
Let others of the rain despair;
It is an answer to the prayer
    Of Squilililigee."

Therefore he climbed his favorite tree
The day the flood was set to be,
    And waited patiently;
He gulped a sob in his little throat
As others rushed to Noah's boat.
    Poor Squilililigee!

Let us not look as the waters rise
To cover his feet and mouth and eyes
    So steadily;
And let our laughter be refined
Whenever his image comes to mind—
    Poor little Squilililigee.

# THE SLEEPAMITEMORE

This sign was always on the door
Behind which slept the Sleepamitemore:

"Just one more wink, one little nap,
Another dip in the slumber stream;
I'm such a sleepy, sleepy chap;
I'm having such a pleasant dream.
Please do not shake me,
Please, please, don't wake me
With whistle, bell, or silver chime,
And please return some other time."

Within, a round and fuzzy ball,
No matter what the hour might be,
The laziest animal of all
Continued sleeping endlessly.

He had no friends, which was no wonder;
For louder than a clap of thunder
There issued forth his mighty snore
That shook the world from shore to shore;
And not a beast was there so brave
Who dared come near that dreadful cave.

Strange tales were told of his aspect,
But these were not at all correct,
Since not a soul, for real and true,
Was speaking from a point of *view!*

Some said, "The lion's tame to *him!*"
Said some, "He's like a dragon grim;
He's rivers wide and mountains high,
And flames shoot out from mouth and eye."

(But all he was was laziness,
And nothing was he more, nor less.)

Each week for minutes just a score,
The latch was lifted from his door,
As out on fat and shuffling feet,
The lazy beast came forth to eat.

Thus once in passing Noah spied
Him munching on a tender herb;
"Our dragon's toothless," Noah cried,

"There's not a mouse he could disturb.
This gentle creature must not perish;
Into my Ark I must ensnare him;
My duty is this beast to cherish,
And from the flood's destruction spare him."

Brave Noah, with no hesitation,
Knocked loudly on the bolted door—
Unanswered, shoved his invitation
Beneath a cranny in the floor.
The drowsy one was furious,
But till his visitor departed
Lay quietly, then curious
Arose, and at the letter darted.
At what he read he was delighted.
His eyes grew wider more and more,
For he had never been invited
To take an ocean trip before.

He read that letter many times,
Until its meaning rang like chimes
Within his fastly nodding head;
And as he nodded, still he read.
The nods grew fewer, weaker, stopped;
His head upon his bosom dropped,
And soon he was asleep once more,
And as he slept a great ship bore
Him (dreaming still) far into space
To many a strange and foreign place.

It was a lovely dream he had,
An ideal dream. *It was too bad
He thought he must continue dreaming!*

He never heard the water streaming
In torrents on the forest floor,
Nor heard the Ark shove off from shore.

Perhaps he still is there, asleep,
In spite of currents cool and deep;
Perhaps that warning, as before,
Still dangles from his cavern door:
"Just one more wink, one little nap,
Another dip in the slumber stream;
I'm such a sleepy, sleepy chap.
I'm having such a pleasant dream."

# THE TREASURETIT

All things lost could now be found,
Though buried fathoms underground,
If only one Treasuretit had been
Dragged to the Ark and hustled in.
All pirate gold, and silver rings,

Pieces of eight and two-penny bits
We could discover, and live like kings,
If we could find some Treasuretits.

Why, we could dress like Indian princes,
Wear silver buckles on our breeches,
And dine on chocolates and quinces.
There'd be no beggars down in ditches,
Nor any man without his coat,
If a Treasuretit had reached the boat!

In truth he was a funny thing,
Quite small and slender, like a stick,
But faster than a bird on wing;
Whoever caught *him* had to be . . . *quick!*

But once in hand, you gripped his tail,
And swung him gently fro and to,
And he was never known to fail
Whoever this magic ditty knew:

"Treasuretit, bright in heat or frost,
Find the precious thing I've lost.
Follow it high, follow it low;
Point me to places treasures go.
Down in ground,
Up in tree,
All around,
Carry me!
Lead me through bush into cave and den,
Follow the thing I've lost, and when
Its hiding place you surely know,
Shine, Treasuretit, oh, shine and glow!"

And as sure as snuff will make you sneeze,
And L. E. Phants weight more than Fleas,
The wee small beastie in your hand,
Would turn and point at this command,
And tug and pull and strain and strive
With every nerve and sense alive;

And many a mile perhaps you'd go,
This way and that, and to and fro,
Across a river and up a mountain,
Down a valley and through a fountain,
And bruised you'd be, and tired and tossed,
But nearer and nearer the thing you lost;
Till Treasuretit would suddenly glow
Like a rod of fire, and then you'd know
That overhead or underground
Whatever you lost was surely found.

Oh why, oh why, didn't *one* embark?
Why didn't one, just *one*, reach the Ark?
For then your dog could find his bone,
Christopher Cat his rubber ball,[1]
Mother could find the precious stone
That slipped through a hole in the garden wall,
And not a single girl or boy
Would ever weep for a mislaid toy.
But human traits we sometimes find
To large degree in animal kind,

[1] **CHRISTOPHER:** It's an *old, old* ball;
It isn't nice at all;
And if I had a Treasuretit,
I wouldn't go in search of it!

And things of greatest worth and use
Are often subject to abuse.

And such, I'm sorry to relate,
Accounts for Treasuretit's sad fate.
He had no quiet, he had no peace;
His life was one continual quest.
If, tired at length, he sought release
In sleep, they yanked him from his nest.
The silly things they made him seek
Could not be told you in a week!
The forest babies, just for spite,
Would wander off into the night,
And burrow deep in bog or pit,
Just to make work for Treasuretit!
Nothing was nailed or held securely.
Let it be lost! All knew that surely
Nothing could harm or happen it;
It would be found by Treasuretit!

How he hated that magic ditty:
"Down in ground,
Up in tree,
All around,
Carry me!"
How he longed for peace and pity!

And how those two for the Ark's trip chosen,
With horror at the thought were frozen!
Oh, what a dismal, dreary fate
Theirs was, they shook to contemplate.
Thousands of animals would be there,
And they of their kind the only pair!

Millions of things would go astray,
And who would find them? They, only they!
They'd have no time to dance or sing,
Or play, or rest, or anything!

They looked ahead . . . and forty days . . .
They looked ahead . . . and forty nights . . .
Of work and weariness met their gaze,
A future stripped of all delights.
Though every passenger might pretend
He was their one and only friend,
Behind this friendliness would lurk
Only the wish to make them work!
The prospect pleased them not a whit;
That's why we have no Treasuretit![1]

---

[1] CHRISTOPHER: For what do you think that those two did
The night before they should embark?
They scampered off into the dark,
And safely and securely hid!

# THE HOODINKUS-WITH-THE DOUBLE-HEAD, OR JUST HOODINKUS

How often have you heard it said
That if you had an extra head,
You might be twice as wise?
How often have you placed your skull
Against a friend's, and tried to pull
An answer from the skies?

One hand is *not* as good as two;
One foot would never, never do;
One eye; how sad a fate!
But when Hoodinkus' history
You hear, I'm sure you will agree
One *head* is adequate.

How shall we best describe this creature?
Two heads were his most striking feature;
One at each end was seen;
And like a long accordion,
His striped body rippled on
In little pleats between.

At first each head tried hard to smother
The envy it felt of the other,
And both were *so* polite.
But all who saw them only waited
Until this courtesy abated;
There *had* to be a fight!

Too soon the disagreement came;
It centered in their choice of name.
"By what name shall we link us?"
"Hoodinkus-With-The-Double-Head,"
Cried one: "Too long!" the other said;
"Why not just . . . 'Hoodinkus?'"

And thus whoever near them came
Must call each head its special name,
Which was a bit of bother;
You couldn't greet them in a hurry;

You greeted one, then had to scurry
Around and greet the other.

Whatever way the animal went,
One head alone could be content;
The other head must nurse
Its disappointment and its wrath
The while it churned a dusty path
Traveling in reverse!

Thus more and more disputes arose
As stubbornly each rival chose
Its way, and would not yield.
For days and days they might not stir,
(Each vowing never to defer!)
Out of some glade or field,

Till in the end the weight of slumber
One head would finally encumber;
And then, so stealthily,
The wide-awake would turn and peep,
Then drag the other, sound asleep,
Away in victory.

But as their body older grew,
The heads, their wisdom adding to,
Had learned to quarrel less,
And had for many years contrived,
Until a certain note arrived,
To live in peacefulness.

They eyed the letter for a while;
Each with a most respectful smile

Upon the other waited;
And would be waiting still I fear,
But luckily they chanced to *hear*
The news the letter *stated.*

"How nice!" the first head beamed, "a trip!
Just think of it, and on a ship!"
Oh, then as if to slaughter
His former friend, the other turned.
His voice with horror blared and burned,
"You know I hate the water!"

"We'll go," the first head spoke, "that's that."
With contradiction full and flat,
The other said, "Not me!
I take my firm and final stand
Where I was born, here on the land;
I'll never go to sea!"

For days on end the quarrel raged;
They were so busily engaged
In their disputing,
They never felt the first drop fall,
They heeded not the Ark's last call,
Nor heard its whistle tooting![1]

----

[1] CHRISTOPHER: From which we learn that headed double,
We'd all be headed straight for trouble
To perish in the rains;
Unless each mortal double-headed
Found both his heads securely wedded
To a triple set of brains.

# THE LAPALAKES

We're at a loss how to describe
This very quaint and curious tribe.
When born they were as small as mice,
But might in time grow larger twice
Than any beast the forest knew;
And often, waddling two by two,
They loomed like mountains tumbling down
Upon some hapless little town.

But not from eating be it known
Had they to these dimensions grown;
Their appetites were small, but thirst!
Of all things thirsty they were first!

The more they drank, the more they craved;
No stream of water might be saved
Which lay in the path of a Lapalake.
In panting hordes they marched to slake
Their thirst at every brook and well;
From lake to lake, from stream to stream,
They drank their way as in a dream.

And this is true, though strange to tell,
Not one of them was known, I think,
Ever to have enough to drink,
Because, to be quite true and candid,
Each had a stomach which *expanded.*

So they, on reading Noah's letter,
Rejoiced that earth would soon be wetter;
No bit of news could please them better.
Their leader spoke, "At any rate,
*Our* tribe will send no delegate
To stifle on his stuffy bark.
What need have we of Noah's Ark?
If, as he says, it's bound to pour,
The place for us is here on shore.
Welcome sweet flood! At last I think
We all shall have enough to drink!"

In line, like soldiers, eye to eye,
They kept their gaze upon the sky;

And as the clouds grew dark with rain,
They scarcely could their joy retain;
And when there fell the first large drop,
Like one they ran to lap it up![1]

A mighty army set in motion,
They drank their way straight to the ocean.
To such a size all soon were bloated,
That on the waves their bodies floated.
Though all around them others sank,
They floated on, and drank and drank.
The rain fell fast, but they drank faster,
Almost they proved the water's master,
And nearly caused a great disaster.

For as they drank and larger grew,
The Fish beneath them had no view
Of anything but Lapalakes.
In awful fright and consternation,
The King Fish said, "For Goodness' Sakes!
I'll have to call a convocation.
These Lapalakes will be our death;
The little air we need for breath
They keep from us," the King Fish said.
"If nothing's done we'll all be dead,
And what a silly kind of slaughter,
For Fish to perish *in the water!*"

"What shall we do?" the King Fish sighed,
But not a single Fish replied.
And not a Fish there raised his head,

[1] CHRISTOPHER: Their jaws flew wider than a well
To catch the water as it fell!

71

But quaking all in fear and dread,
Each stole a shy glance at the Whale,
But even he was somewhat pale.

"Live long, King Fish!" Whose voice is this
Which from afar fills all with bliss?
Who comes in gay and glittering line,
A thousand strong, cleaving the brine?
The Swordfish clan, till then delayed,
Before their King their homage paid.
"Live long, O King! That you *may* live,
We mount above our lives to give,"
Their leader cried. "No Lapalake
Shall from our King his kingdom take!"

Each swordfish then, as one, drew out
The mighty sword which was his snout,
And upward sped with battle shout.
A sharp thrust here, a sharp thrust there,
And loud explosions filled the air![1]

[1] CHRISTOPHER: And quicker than the telling takes,
That was the end of the Lapalakes!

# THE SNAKE-THAT-WALKED-
UPON-HIS-TAIL

How envied, how admired a male,
The-Snake-That-Walked-Upon-His-Tail!
The forest all emerged to stare
When he came out to take the air.
With bright eye flashing merrily,
He seemed to say, "Come, gaze on me!

Behold as near as animal's can,
A walk resembling that of man!"
And holding high his haughty head,
He would stroll on with graceful tread.
And how his tiny little ear
Would throb these compliments to hear:
"What charm he has!" "What elegance!"
"The ideal partner for a dance!"
"However do you think he learned?"
At this, although he blushed and burned
To tell them how, he never turned,
But, looking neither left nor right,
Would wander on and out of sight.

But why indeed was he so gifted?
By what strange powers was he lifted
A little nearer to the skies?
The reason's plain. Hard exercise!
Hard exercise, indeed! You shake
Your head, and think, "When did a snake,
A creature sleepy and inert,
Content to slumber in the dirt,
Or lie in caverns dank and dark,
Exhibit such a worthy spark?"

But be it found in man or horse,
(Or even snake) a driving force
The fever is we call ambition.
When it attacks, there's no condition
Of man or beast which may withstand
Ambition's hard, compelling hand.

And from his very, very birth,
No common snake was this of ours;
But he was conscious of his worth,
And well aware of all his powers.
He never cared for toads and newts,
For catching flies or digging roots;
No cavern cool could lure him in,
No muddy bank his fancy win.
Wherever man was, there was he!
Eager to watch, eager to see!
He thought it fine that Man could talk,
But finer still that Man could *walk*.
He thought, "If Man can do this, why
With proper training, so can I."

He kept his secret from his nearest
Friend, he never told his dearest,
But in a quiet glade he knew
Where none was apt to come and spy,
The more his perseverance grew,
The nearer did his dream draw nigh;
He practiced patiently and drilled,
And *wished*, and *yearned*, and *longed*, and *willed*.
From crack of dawn to darkest night,
He practiced sitting bolt upright.
At first he fell with a terrible thump,
And bruised his head and raised a bump;
But, "Walk I will!" is what he said,
And lightly rubbed his aching head.

Night after night, day after day,
He would sit up, and sway and sway,
Until one day, oh, think of it!
He stood and never swayed a bit!
He stood as rigid as a pole,
With perfect ease, perfect control!

Though Men should do most wondrous things
In years to come: on iron wings
Fly faster than the fastest bird,
Or talk or sing, and make it heard
Over mountains and over seas,
You must confess that none of these
Could for excitement quite compare
With Snake triumphant standing there
Tiptoe upon his tail! And now
How to begin? He wondered how!
What should he do? Leap? Jump? Or stride?
His heart was hammering inside
Its narrow cell! His throat was dry!
Ambition's fever fired his eye.
Within his grasp he had his dream.
Here was his moment, his, supreme!

Just then he chanced to glance and see
Man passing by, most leisurely;
Step after step Man took with ease,
Eclipsing houses, rocks, and trees.
And suddenly our Snake grew pale,
And whimpered forth a woeful wail;
Till Doomsday though he stood on end,
He would not walk! No need pretend!
One thing he lacked to be complete.
Nothing could walk which hadn't *feet!*

Down, down, he dropped, and sadly crept
Into a bush nearby, and wept.
The tears he shed were sad and salty;
He felt a failure, weak and faulty.
At last, too weary more to weep,
He curled him up and went to sleep.

But some sweet spirit knew his zeal,
Pitied his grief, and sped to heal.
Our Snake's ambitious lower tip
Was caught in some magician's grip,
Till where had been, so sharp and neat,
A tail, were now two tiny feet.
It may have been by wishing so
His earnestness had made them grow!
At any rate, as I repeat,
When he awoke, there were his feet!

He wept again, but now for pleasure!
His joy burst forth in lavish measure.
He popped up straighter than an arrow;
Happiness went bubbling through his marrow!

Then gingerly and cautiously,
And praying Heaven kind to be,
He put his best foot forward! Oh,
It knew exactly where to go!
Without the slightest fuss or bother
Straight behind it came the other.
And from that day until his fall,
He was a wonder to them all.

Pray notice well that last remark,
To wit: "Until his fall," for hark

How too much pride and too much glory
Bring dismal climax to our story.
Our hero, for I still opine
That such he was, though serpentine,
Waxed fat on praise and admiration,
Forgot his former lowly station,
Looked on his mate with mild disdain
As being somewhat soft of brain;

With favor viewed her not at all,
Because, poor thing, she still must *crawl!*
(Which needs no explanation here,
For we believe we've made it clear
That of these two only the Male
Contrived to walk upon his tail.)

The compliments which, left and right,
Were showered on him, spoiled him quite;
No longer friendly and benign,
He strode along with rigid spine,
Nor bent to pass the time of day
Though gently greeted on the way.
Himself he thought the world's last wonder
All other beasts a foolish blunder,
And even Man he somewhat eyed
A bit obliquely in his pride.

One only thing, or rather two,
He loved with ardor all complete;
Yea, evermore his rapture grew
As he beheld his darling feet!
He bathed them in the coolest brooks,
Wrapped them in leaves against the heat;

He never wearied of the looks
Of those amazing little feet!
And every day, foul day or fair,
Most carefully did count his toes
To be quite certain they were there,
Two sets of five, in double rows.

Flood morning came and Mrs. Snake
Was early up and wide awake.
"Dear husband, rise," she hissed, "the Ark
We must be on and in ere dark."
But he, he only stretched and yawned,
As in his brain an idea dawned
That promised great publicity.
"Suppose, my dear, you go," said he,
"Ahead, and wait on board for me.
Your rate of travel's none too great.
You crawl along; I won't be late."

"True," said Madam, somewhat tartly,
"I travel as the good Lord made me;
And though I may not travel smartly,
My crawling never has delayed me."
At which in somewhat of a huff,
She straightened out and rippled off.

Quite tardily our Snake arose,
Sat fondly gazing at his toes,
And thought, "The last to catch the boat
I'll be; arrive as one of note.
Perhaps its sailing I'll delay
Almost as much as one whole day;
For certainly they wouldn't dare
To sail away with me not there."

Through all the bustle and commotion
Of others hastening to the ocean,
He gaily spent his time in primping
And polishing his shiny scales,
And laughed to think of others limping
Instead of walking on their tails.

Long, long he dillied, long, long he dallied,
And dilly-dalliers never yet
Have at the proper moment sallied
To where they were supposed to get.
At length he deemed the proper second
For his departure had appeared;
The fame of being latest beckoned;
For conquest he felt fully geared.

But even as he straightly rose,
And lightly turned upon his toes,
The quiet skies above him darkened.
A panic seized him as he harkened
To thunder rolling long and loud.
Foreboding filled his frame, and dread,
As, glancing up, he saw a cloud
About to spill its contents on his head!
He fled in fright; away he scurried;
From that disturbing spot he hurried.
Yet ever as he onward sped
That cloud still threatened overhead.

At last, at last, he nears the Ark;
'Tis just a little ways away!
Its lights are gleaming in the dark,
It rocks with laughter loud and gay.

"Oh, let me reach it," gasps our hero;
"Though fame and fortune be as zero,
Though none my praises sing aloud,
O Heaven, spare me from that cloud!"

What irony of fate is this?
What bitter fare is his to eat?
Why does our hero writhe and hiss?
Something has tangled up his feet.
A little plant, a sickly bush,
Has grappled with those lovely toes;
Though he may flounder, shove, and push,
No further on our hero goes.
The awful cloud above him tips
And pours its mighty torrents down.
One last look and the captive slips
Away within their depths to drown.
Undone by what he loved the most
He gently renders up the ghost.

Long may his mate stand at the rail,
With anxious eye explore the dark;
The-Snake-That-Walked-Upon-His-Tail
Will never walk upon the Ark.[1]

---

[1] CHRISTOPHER: And never, never in any Zoo
         Excite the wonderment of you!

# THE HA-HA-HA

Oh, merry, merry, merry, merry,
And very, very, very, very
Amusing was the Ha-Ha-Ha.
"Tra-la," he sang, "Tra-la-la-la."

His like for friskiness and mirth,
No more will walk upon our earth;

From morning break till evening light,
He clutched his stomach fast and tight,
And found some cause for merriment
In every small or large event.

Oh, merry was the Ha-Ha-Ha.
"Tra-la," he sang, "Tra-la-la-la."

Each morn he woke with sparkling eyes,
Glad of the day, glad of the skies;
And all his wits at once were bent
On mischief-making merriment.
Where'er he strolled great crowds came after,
For they were sure of fun and laughter.

So funny was the Ha-Ha-Ha;
"Tra-la," he sang, "Tra-la-la-la."

Though you might guess, you never knew
What next the Ha-Ha-Ha would do;
Oh, countless were the pranks he played
In many a dashing escapade;
Why, once he grasped L. E. Phant's snout,
And swung it round and round about!

So daring was the Ha-Ha-Ha;
"Tra-la," he sang "Tra-la-la-la."

Round as a wreath of Christmas holly,
There never was a beast so jolly,
Nor one who found life such a jest!
He laughed the buttons from his vest,
The spectacles laughed from his nose,
And all the toenails from his toes!

So merry was the Ha-Ha-Ha;
"Tra-la," he sang, "Tra-la-la-la."

So holding Noah's note in hand,
He rocked with laughter as he scanned
This warning of the coming rain.
"Rain forty days! The man's insane!
Of such a thing whoever heard?
It's too fantastic and absurd!"

So said the merry Ha-Ha-Ha.
"Tra-la," he sang, "Tra-la-la-la."

"There's not a cloud so large and high
It wouldn't be completely dry
In seven days (at most a week!)[1]
But forty days! Does Noah seek
To prove us all devoid of brains
With all this talk of floods and rains?"

Indignant was the Ha-Ha-Ha.
"Tra-la," he scoffed, "Tra-la-la-la."

The Ha-Ha-Has thus, all and each,
With lively, laughing, mocking speech
Their neighbors dubbed soft and demented,
With heads, they said, too quickly dented,
And woefully in need of brains
With this belief in floods and rains.

[1] CHRISTOPHER: The Ha-Ha-Ha was in a daze,
For what's a week but seven days?

A skeptic was the Ha-Ha-Ha.
"Tra-la," he jeered, "Tra-la-la-la."

The Ha-Ha-Has themselves forgot
(It was their purpose so to do)
To draw a straw, or cast a lot,
Appoint, elect, or choose their two—
As stubbornly these scoffers went
On blithely making merriment.

Still merry was the Ha-Ha-Ha.
"Tra-la," he sang, "Tra-la-la-la."

With smiling face and twinkling eye,
They watched their fellows bustling by,
Through thicket, grass, and rustling sedge,
Down and away to the water's edge.
Down and away, and up the plank,
Beast after beast, rank after rank.

"How silly," quoth the Ha-Ha-Ha.
"Tra-la," he trilled, "Tra-la-la-la."

The Ha-Ha-Has, as the first drops fell,
All smiled, and thought, "How fine and well
For grass and flower and thirsty tree
This passing shower is bound to be;
All ripening things will bud and bloom
With richer, heavier perfume."

Full happy was the Ha-Ha-Ha.
"Tra-la," he sang, "Tra-la-la-la."

For one long day and one whole night,
They watched it rain and felt no fright;
For two long nights and three long days
They still retained their merry ways,
But after a week of pitter-patter,
They found the rain no laughing matter!

Then sober was the Ha-Ha-Ha,
Though still he sang, "Tra-la-la-la."

From tree to tree, from rock to rock,
Their spirits damp, the weary flock
Of Ha-Ha-Has essayed in vain
To reach a spot exempt from rain.
But neither tree, nor rock, nor mountain
Gave refuge from that steady fountain.

And drowned was every Ha-Ha-Ha,
Though singing still, "Tra-la-la-la."

Away, away, so far away,
There safely, lightly, on the spray,
With lights aglow before and aft,
Rode Noah's homely little craft.
Gay though it was, it would have been
Much gayer with a Ha-Ha- in.[1]

All missed the merry Ha-Ha-Ha.
All missed his merry "Tra-la-la."

[1] CHRISTOPHER: To make our rhyme and rhythm fit,
The extra Ha we must omit.

Though gay and glad our world is still,
The laughter lost we never will
In fullest measure know again
That left our earth forever when,
Caught in the waters perilous,
The Ha-Ha-Has were snatched from us.

So merry, merry, merry, merry,
And very, very, very, very
Amusing was the Ha-Ha-Ha;
"Tra-la," he sang, "Tra-la-la-la."

# MORE ABOUT CHRISTOPHER

Just as the Ha-Ha-Ha's last "tra-la-la-la" had faded away into the thinnest whisper of an echo, it came to me with a sudden shock that here was our story all complete, but that two of our animals had been entirely overlooked.

"But, Christopher," I asked, "what about the Pussybow?"

"Pussybow?" answered Christopher. "What on earth is that?"

"Don't you remember, Christopher? You know (and here I began to quote) 'The Pussybow that could mew and bark.' Don't you remember him? We've left him out altogether."

"I don't know anything about him," denied Christopher. "I never heard of him before. The name itself sounds perfectly silly; Pussybow indeed!" And here he gave one of those little cat sneezes which are always a warning that he is about to be disagreeable and quarrel-some.

"Christopher, how can you sit there, twirling your whiskers in such a self-satisfied and conceited way, looking me calmly in the eye as you are doing, and tell me that you never heard of the Pussybow?" I cried.

"But I never did!" he insisted.

Thoroughly peeved and determined to show that a cat cannot make a monkey of me, I gathered up our story, thumbed it through from beginning to end, and back again, until I finally located the line about the Pussybow.

"There!" I exclaimed. " 'The Pussybow that could mew and bark!' " In triumph I waved the line under Christopher's nose with such force that he turned a double-somersault trying to escape the telltale sheet of paper.

"That," argued my stubborn cat, "proves absolutely nothing. The mere fact that you have discovered your own reference to such a thing as the Pussybow doesn't prove that it was me, or rather I, that told you about it. It's certainly no more than a creature of your own wild imagination. Now, let's be reasonable about this matter." (Here he drew a little nearer to me, but he still kept a fair distance away, fearing perhaps that my temper might get beyond my control in the course of this conversation.) "From what you say about this, this Pussybow, that is that he could mew and bark at the same time, I imagine that he must have been a compound of cat and dog. Now what could be sillier than that? There could have been, and there *was* a twelve-eyed Wakeupworld. There's nothing impossible about such an animal. There could have been and there *was* a Double-Headed Hoodinkus and a Treasuretit, and there certainly could have been a

Squilililigee! But a Pussybow! That's the most ridiculous and fantastic animal I ever heard of! There wouldn't be any reason for such an animal. Since there were already cats of the finest type, and dogs, too (fine enough in the limited way of dogs), what good could have come of having half a dog and half a cat? No, my good master (this was made to sound like affection, but I detected in it the worst kind of sarcasm), the Pussybow has never lived anywhere except in your imagination, and I think it best that we leave him there."

Christopher has always been a more impressive talker than I, and much against my will I found myself absolutely speechless before him, as I pondered over what he had said. The more I thought the matter over, the more I began to feel that he was right. I couldn't for the life of me recall any exact moment in his story when he had said anything about a Pussybow. His other animals had charmed me so that I must have unwittingly invented the Pussybow myself.

And now I had to apologize. Oh, yes, I knew I had that to do, no matter how distasteful it might be. For there Christopher sat, patiently waiting. He knew that he was in the right, and he also knew that well-mannered humans always apologize when in the wrong. So there he sat, looking at me with twinkling eyes, and now and then giving his really magnificent whiskers an extra twirl. He'd never turn away and simply forget the whole thing. Oh, no, he'd wait until he had his apology.

I might as well get it over.

"Christopher," I began timidly, for you have no idea how difficult it is to apologize to a cat.

"Yes?" said Christopher, and his frigid tone and I-told-you-so look didn't make my task any easier.

"I'm sorry," I blurted out as fast as I could. "You're right and I'm wrong. I'm convinced that you never told me a word about the Pussybow. I must have invented him. I'm sorry, and I apologize."

"Your apology is accepted," Christopher purred, as he arched his back higher than usual and waved his tail in triumph, "but I can't help saying that if you and the general run of humankind thought twice before speaking once, you'd probably make fewer mistakes and have fewer reasons for always going around apologizing to one another."

Having said this in a most school-teacherish manner, he started out to leave me to myself, doubtless deeming it a great punishment for me to be deprived of his company.

However, there was still another mystery to be solved, and just as the tip of his tail was about to vanish over the doorsill, I called him.

"Christopher," I called, my voice sounding very sorrowful and pleading, "please come back."

The words were scarcely out of my mouth before he was back and over the sill, rubbing against my leg and purring like a kettle seven days heating. He hadn't wanted to leave the room at all, for he knew perfectly well that I was the only one in the house able to talk to him. And by now he had begun to enjoy this business of talking. It really made him a cat apart.

"Would you like me to mail the book for you?" he wanted to know. He was just being smart and putting on airs, for he knew very well that the postmaster couldn't speak cat.

"No," I answered, just as if he could have mailed the book, because I didn't want to upset him again too soon. "Not yet, because there's one more point to clear up."

"I do hope," he said with a sigh, "that it isn't something else as ridiculous as your imaginary Pussybow."

"I hope not, too," I answered, trying hard to keep him in a good humor as long as possible. "But what about the Lizard, Christopher?"

"The Lizard?" he wanted to know.

"Yes, Christopher, the Lopsided Lizard?"

"The Lopsided Lizard?" he repeated after me, as if we were playing a game of you say it and then I say it.

"Yes, Christopher, in fact the *One-sided* Lopsided Lizard is what you called him. You remember telling me about him, don't you? He *was* one of the lost animals, wasn't he?"

"Yes," Christopher replied, a little slowly it seemed to me, "I remember telling you about him."

"What about him, then? You'll have to describe him to me, and tell me why he didn't get into the Ark so I can write about him just as I did about the others."

"The truth is," confessed Christopher finally, "that I've forgotten just what he looked like, and just what he did to prevent his getting into the Ark."

"The truth is, Christopher," I accused him, "that I don't believe there ever was a *One-sided* Lopsided Lizard. He's just as much a creature of your imagination as the Pussybow was of mine. In the first place, he might have been *lopsided*, but he couldn't have been *one-sided*."

"Just why couldn't he have been *one-sided*, as my father told me he was?" demanded Christopher sulkily.

"Nothing can be one-sided," I tried to explain. "There just must be two sides to everything, no matter how thin it is."

"I don't believe it," said Christopher flatly. "My father

93

always said the One-sided Lopsided Lizard, so it must have been one-sided."

"Come, come, Christopher," I said, "don't be exasperating, and don't act like a silly kitten which hasn't had time to open his eyes to the world around him. You're too old for that. I'll prove to you that your old lizard couldn't have been one-sided. Now, what's the thinnest thing you can think of?"

Christopher thought a moment, and then said, "One of the hairs out of my whiskers."

"Fine!" I agreed. "Let me have one."

"Take it," he said, rising on his hind legs and stretching up to me.

"No, you give me one," I said. "It won't hurt so much if you pull it out yourself."

Without so much as an ouch, he reached up and pulled out a very fine and silvery hair which he handed over to me.

"Now look here, Christopher," I explained patiently, "can't you see that even as thin as this hair is, nobody could call it *one-sided*? It has to have two sides. And I'm sure your Lopsided Lizard was broader than this."

How stubborn that cat can be!

"I don't see but *one side to that hair*," he argued, "and my father always said that lizard was *one-sided*; and furthermore I don't thank you for saying that my father didn't know what he was talking about."

That last remark caught me entirely off guard.

"I never said anything about your father, Christopher," I protested. "I never mentioned your father at all."

"Not openly, you didn't," Christopher agreed heatedly, "but you might just as well accuse him of not telling the truth as deny that there could be a One-sided Lopsided Lizard!"

Now, there I was caught again. It didn't seem to me, by all the laws of reason, that there ever could have been such an animal as a One-sided Lopsided Lizard. Christopher couldn't remember what his father had said the Lizard looked like, nor what had happened to him at the time of the flood, but he was still going to hold out that there could have been one.

Determined not to do any more apologizing, I took my hat and went for a walk (even though it was raining!), leaving Christopher at home to sulk alone.

The more I thought about it, the more that Lizard worried me. How I should like to know (if there really were such a thing) what that One-sided Lopsided Lizard looked like, and why he didn't get into the Ark! Was he too slow to keep up with the rest of the animals? Or, since he was lopsided (and *one-sided* according to Christopher), did each hop or jump he took take him further away from the Ark instead of nearer to it? I'd really like to know. Maybe some boy or girl reading this book can tell me. It may be that one of you has a pet Dannie Dog, or a Michael Monkey, or a little Leonard Lamb whose ancestors were on the Ark just as Christopher's were. And maybe you can get your pet to tell you the story of the One-sided Lopsided Lizard. If so, Christopher and I would like very much to know.

And maybe there was a Pussybow, too.